THE LEADER'S GUIDE
TO RECAPTURING
THE TRUST

This book was designed to be used alone or as
a companion to the online training program
A Leaders Guide to Recapturing the Trust
(www.recapturingthetrust.com)

The online program has been created for those who prefer
an interactive experience which is highly active as well,
providing opportunities to assess, learn, and apply what
has been learned. Action plans at the end of each online
unit include practical solutions which may be applied to
the users' specific situations.

Trust is like a butterfly, capricious and delicate.
To capture a butterfly
one has to use a soft net and a gentle touch.

THE LEADER'S GUIDE TO RECAPTURING THE TRUST

50 Years of Declining Trust in
American Organizations
and What You Can Do about It

Robert Schachat, PhD

iUniverse, Inc.
New York Lincoln Shanghai

THE LEADER'S GUIDE TO RECAPTURING THE TRUST
50 Years of Declining Trust in American Organizations and What You Can Do about It

iUniverse, Inc.

For information address:
iUniverse
2021 Pine Lake Road, Suite 100
Lincoln, NE 68512
www.iuniverse.com

ISBN: 0-595-28765-4

Printed in the United States of America

FOREWORD

In 1999, after nearly thirty years of battling trust wars in over two hundred organizations, I wrote *Recapturing the Trust—50 Years of Declining Trust in American Organizations and What You Can Do about It.* This book reflected my research and experiences related to what I saw as Americans' declining trust in their institutions, especially their business organizations.

I enjoyed a modest, yet not unexpected, amount of attention to my findings and recommendations. Everyone considered "trust" to be an important issue, but no more so than any of the other relationship issues affecting organizational image and success.

Suddenly, in 2002, in the midst of accounting and corporate scandals, the public's clamor and outrage brought the concept of "trust and integrity" to the forefront, and it became the catchphrase of seemingly every commentary and analysis of American business.

Having been an executive coach for senior officers in some of the headlined companies, I had an intimate understanding of why and how these bubbles burst. As a result, I felt compelled to spend the summer of 2002 reinterviewing the dozens of executives whom I had quoted and whose ideas I had cited in my book, along with a host of other leaders from some of the most embattled firms. I also met with fellow management consultants and business professors, and I spoke with representatives of consumer and investor groups—business stakeholders who have become more vocal and influential than ever before regarding their feelings and demands concerning trust and American corporate governance.

As additional scandals emerged and public outrage intensified, Congress responded with the Sarbanes-Oxley Act of 2002, a serious update of the laws governing corporate fraud and other "white collar crime."

The regulations emanating from the law call for mandatory codes of ethics, investor safeguards, and reformed accounting practices; and inherent in these dictates is training for the officers of publicly traded companies. Too many of these companies have lost the trust among their employees that would enable the kind of feedback required to *discuss* potential ethical dilemmas, no less to confront or challenge illegal or unethical acts or intentions to act.

One form of training mandated by the Sarbanes-Oxley Act involves ethical behavior. Ethics will flourish in an environment of trust. In order to comply with the letter and spirit of the new law, public companies must instill ethics and trust by encouraging the giving and receiving of feedback and fostering two-way inter-personal communication throughout the organization.

So acting with trust and integrity is now more than just good business, it's the law. And paradoxically, without trust, any efforts to legally mandate appropriate organizational conduct or create ethical dialog will fail.

This book, with its simple audit/assessments and step-by-step solutions provides the leadership concepts and skills which will enable you to create and maintain an environment of trust through the effective management, coaching, and mentoring of today's workforce in today's organizations. You will learn how to be an agent of trust, fostering and modeling trust-building behaviors. You will also learn and acquire the behaviors of a trusted coach, a trusted business mentor, and a trusted visionary, while affirming the integrity of your leadership and your organization.

CONTENTS

ACKNOWLEDGEMENTS xiii

GETTING STARTED 1
THE SEVEN CONDITIONS OF TRUST 4
    Freedom from Fear 4
    Non-Deceptive Intentions 5
    Role Clarity 7
    Risk Taking 8
    Mutuality and Sharing 10
    Task-Related Competence 11
    Interpersonal Sensitivity 12
    The Seven Conditions–Summing Up 13
CHARACTERISTICS OF GREAT LEADERS 14
THE YEARS OF DECLINING TRUST 15
    The Organizational Climate 1945–1960 15
    The Organizational Climate 1960–1980 16
    The Organizational Climate 1980–TODAY 16
    The Organizational Climate–Conclusion 17
THOUGHT QUESTIONS 18

UNIT ONE THE LEADER AS AGENT OF TRUST 19
    Assessing Coworker Behaviors 19
    The Johari Window 21
    Interpersonal Charisma 24
    Assessing Your Supervisor 26

Assessing Your Organization 28
Assessing the Public's Perception of Trust 30
CONCLUSION 32

UNIT TWO THE LEADER AS COACH 33
THE FUNDAMENTAL SKILLS FOR EFFECTIVE
INTERPERSONAL COMMUNICATIONS 33
Active Listening 33
Describing and Confirming Behavior 34
Managing Feelings or Personal Reactions 36
APPLYING THE FUNDAMENTAL COMMUNICATION SKILLS 37
Confronting Performance Problems 37
Asking for Feedback from a Defensive Supervisor 38
Dealing with an Attitude or Performance
Concern with a Peer or Subordinate 40
One-on-One Coaching and Counseling 41
CONCLUSION 41

UNIT THREE THE LEADER AS BUSINESS CONSULTANT 43
FACILITATING GROUP PROBLEM-SOLVING 44
The Force-Field Analysis 44
TEAM LEADERSHIP 45
Trust-Building for Teams 45
The Strength Bombardment 47
CONFLICT MEDIATION 47
Do-It-Yourself Mediation 48
Third Party Mediation 48
Managing Conflict between Groups 49
CONCLUSION 50

UNIT FOUR THE LEADER AS VISIONARY 51

SELF-CONCEPT 51

    Work Values 52

    Competency Review 53

LIFE HISTORY RETROSPECTIVE 53

GOALS AND GOAL-SETTING 53

CONCLUSION 54

IN CONCLUSION 55

To A. B. S.

ACKNOWLEDGEMENTS

Thanks to all of the people who played a part in the creation of this book: those friends and colleagues who have encouraged and provoked me to action; the people whom I interviewed and whose words I've proudly spread throughout; the mentors and teachers upon whose shoulders I have gratefully stood in order to see the world as I do.

Thanks to the Mercy College community with its distinguished faculty and staff. Thanks also to its extraordinary student body—unmatched anywhere in its diversity and its salt-of-the-earth pragmatism. My experience there has nurtured my work, providing me with continual support, critique, insight, and intellectual and personal renewal.

Special thanks to Rob Edward, Tom Hopkins, Michael Boyle, and Dianne Job.

GETTING STARTED

As a management consultant and organizational psychologist, my job is finding creative and acceptable ways to provoke trust between and among people…trust that springs not from love or liking necessarily, but from the truth, when its communication is relevant to a business and business relationships. I've always been fascinated by the impact the word "trust" has in all kinds of conversation and situations. Bringing up the topic of trust at work inevitably evokes a variety of strong reactions. After hearing some long and convoluted complaint about an employee, a supervisor, or "management," I tend to get right to the heart of the issue by asking: "Do you trust (him, her, them)?"

A long, telling pause ensues, followed by the admission that, "Well, no, I don't."

How about you? Does the word "trust" provoke a strong reaction? Let's try: answer from 1 to 10 (low to high) the extent to which you trust your supervisor or any one of your direct reports. Do you have what it takes to trust others? On the other hand, to what extent do people in your organization and others in general trust you? Do you have what it takes to enable others to trust you?

This book will help you in all those human interactions where trust plays a vital part—and do you know any in which it doesn't? It will help you consider the impact of your own attitudes about trusting others and enable you to enhance productivity and satisfaction at work. It concerns the role that trust plays in human relations, specifically in the world of work, which consumes so much of our lives. This book also explores how trust has declined in American businesses and organizations, and presents some of the best practices we all can use to reestablish it.

The target of this book is *organizational trust*. It examines a wide variety of circumstances involving trust, focusing on what employers, corporate officers, and supervisors can do and say to encourage and nurture trust among employees.

This book reveals how to influence the quality of your daily work life in your organization and create a productive and meaningful work environment. It also explores the ways to lead for maximum credibility, performance and profitability;

how to restore the good will of your employees, your customers, and your investors; and how to attract and retain today's most promising talent.

"Why would I ever want to tell a colleague how I really feel about them?" is the all-too-common response to my never-end-ing plea to "tell the truth about how you feel with any and all close work associates." Of course you need to have two abilities: first, to say it so that others can "hear" it, and second, to know when and when not to say it. This book will help you to acquire those abilities.

Morale, productivity and profitability within your organization, as well as how your organization is perceived by your customers and investors are all directly related to the level of trust shared by employees and management.

⇨ In *Unit One* you will assess the level of trust among your coworkers, the level of trust inspired by your supervisor, and the level of trust within and for your organization.

⇨ With the knowledge and skills in *Unit Two,* you can become a facilitator of trust in your organization—more persuasive and interpersonally charismatic in order to better coach and mentor peak performance.

⇨ In *Unit Three* you will learn about how to spearhead growth and renewal by helping your people respond to continuous changes.

⇨ In *Unit Four* you will practice the skills involved in visionary leadership—better understanding human behaviors at work and using new insights and skills to motivate and mentor your employees.

The effect of low-trust environments is obvious: they are unhealthy for humans. Low trust in the workplace yields low morale and low creativity. Extensive research over the years has confirmed that because of the resulting compromised productivity, these environments are deadly for the bottom line as well.

People talk. Organizational image and reputation is discussed "on the street" and even in a lean job market, talented candidates will avoid organizations with negative reputations. And with the recent combination of exposed fraud, greed and economic downturn, a wary public of customers, investors, and regulators has become a pack of zealous watchdogs.

But I'm delighted to assert that there is hope. Dysfunctional and trust-eroding behaviors, unconscious and normative though they may have become, can be eliminated by applying the fundamental relationship skills of *effective interpersonal communication* and establishing the *seven conditions of trust.*

Trust is like a butterfly, capricious and delicate. To capture a butterfly, one has to use a soft net and a gentle touch. Throughout this book, I'll present practices we can all use to recapture trust. I use the word "recapture" quite deliberately. Once lost, trust is not quickly rebuilt. For many with whom I've spoken, betrayal of trust is never forgotten nor forgiven.

Determinants such as social norms, personality types, personal histories, and reward systems affect our sensitivity to issues of trust. People's propensity to trust varies as greatly as opinions and temperament; yet even among the most naively trusting of us, once a breach of trust is noticed, trust is slow to come back. When trust escapes, we become detached from others and ourselves. We don't relate emotionally or intellectually, and alienation is the inevitable result.

People in low-trust environments display distinct symptoms:
⇨ Withholding essential information
⇨ Rejecting their commitment to the organization's vision and values
⇨ Talking at and not with one another
⇨ Ignoring the impact that some event may have on an area other than their own
⇨ Treating others as objects to serve a specific purpose
⇨ Committing unethical acts, because detached emotional relationships reinforce short-term self-interest, diminishing the empathy required to see the value in "doing the right thing"

Sound familiar? I'm sure it does. "Lack of communication," "lack of commitment," "lack of teamwork," "lack of leadership" and/or "lack of vision" are among the most often cited laments of the many clients I've worked with in my consulting business. The underlying issue always turns out to be a lack of trust. And, when examined, the associated emotion is a sense of lonely distance and emptiness.

I believe that communication is the antidote to this condition. Communication implies truth—an honesty between people that can be seen and heard in word and in deed. In business, one's word is essential. Whether a person's word is doubted because of purposeful deception or an interpersonal failing in matching one's perceived behavior to one's good intent, the effect is the same: distrust due to another's perception of having been deceived.

Our task is to keep working on the skills that build respect and trust. Being open to giving and receiving feedback about the helpful and the nonhelpful things we say and do are the skills of effective interpersonal communication that will help us and those with whom we interact.

THE SEVEN CONDITIONS OF TRUST

In establishing the underlying philosophy of this book, I interviewed dozens of executives about trust in their organizations. Based on these interviews, I have concluded that there are seven fundamental principals essential to supervisory and organizational trust. These *seven conditions of trust* are: freedom from fear, non-deceptive intentions, role clarity, risk taking, mutuality and sharing, task-related competency, and interpersonal sensitivity.

I have included a sampling of these interviews in the following discussion, to provide a look at how some of these mentors and practitioners in the world of organizations view the seven conditions as they relate to interpersonal relations in the workplace.

Freedom from Fear

At work, most people are afraid much of the time, and fear is dysfunctional. Intimidation paralyzes creativity and productivity. Of the many challenging, provocative, and brilliant suggestions promoted by Edward Demming, the management consultant/industrial psychologist credited with having built the post-war Japanese corporate empire, "driving fear out of the workplace" is one of the best known.

How many times have you sighed with relief on realizing that you weren't caught being late? I used to meet with a very senior-level executive whose behavior proved that movement up the corporate ladder does not necessarily guarantee freedom. At the end of the day, he would listen for sounds and motion in the next office. He would never leave for home until he was sure that his boss had already left for the day.

George Kenney, a former partner and CIO at the Nicholas Applegate Asset Management firm in San Diego, spoke to me about his shift away from an authoritarian fear-inducing management style after his move to southern California:

"I've finally been able to integrate the 'soft side' of management into my otherwise results-driven management style, which, as you know, served me so well back East. At my last position, for example, I would say, 'I have no time for incompetence, nor do I have time for the unfortunates.' Not anymore. Not here, anyway. In this competitive field of Information Technology, we have to practice a more humanistic and trust-oriented approach in order to attract and retain talent."

Kenney reminisced about the old days of intimidation, characterized by "a pit-in-the-stomach" feeling…"We'd always be on guard for a swipe or a snipe…in an organizational culture characterized by blaming, destructive criticism, and competitive jockeying for position."

Does Kenney now feel out of sync with the older, more authoritarian management system? To this question, he remarked, "For some other units and individuals in this and other organizations, this humanistic and collaborative approach may be ill-fitting and dysfunctional, and some people's personality and job requirements may be better suited to control and stress. But, in my service end of the business, people tend to thrive on respect and tranquility."

- ☐ How do you feel about this leader's perception of fear in the workplace and its possible elimination?
- ☐ What in your organization arouses fear?

Non-Deceptive Intentions

Most people at work are wary of being deceived. People tend to remember promises, however cautiously or casually they may have been offered. I believe initial promises are rarely forgotten and—if kept—create strong emotional threads of attraction and retention.

Sloppiness about promises and expectations is a great problem in American business today. Document your promises. For any number of reasons, we all have selective memory. Write out all interpersonal contracts. Written documentation can act to implement deserved rewards while safeguarding the agreement. Broken promises are counterproductive. One of the main reasons why people resist change is their sense that promises used to lure them to new positions or activities will be breached.

And be careful! People tend to collect on broken promises. Employees of a retail client of mine told me of the clever way in which some employee stole in clothing, the equivalent of a broken promise of a bonus that never came. In this situation, the store-owner's greedy and deceptive behavior led to such resentment that the employee was determined to do whatever was felt necessary to even the score.

We trust those who make us believe that they are telling the truth and that they have nothing to hide. Share your motives for your behavior. Trust increases with increased understanding of why someone has chosen a course of action. Unknown motives combined with failure to inspire trust lead to limitless suspicion. Withholding and manipulation, deception, and the suspicion of deception too often lead to mutual duplicity.

Scott Darrah, Human Resource Manager at IBM, has observed lots of "culture change" at his company. No organization is better known than his for the shock of downsizing and the potentially deleterious effects it may have on employee morale and trust.

"The single most important lesson for IBM and all the other organizations who have had to downsize is over-communicate. Give straight talk from the beginning. Communicate more than you think is necessary."

☐ How do you feel about this leader's perceptions of deceptive practices in the workplace and their possible elimination?

☐ How clear is *your* understanding of your organization's mission and values? How well do your policies and strategies support these values?

☐ What value statement do you have regarding integrity or trust, which provides a standard against which your policies and strategies can be measured?

☐ What can be done to better align your organization's mission, vision, and values with those of its employees?

The next time you come to an agreement with a supervisor, peer or subordinate, suggest that the terms be put in writing.

Role Clarity

Trust increases when we share our expectations with another and when that other responds positively to those needs. Most people are incapable of reading others' minds. Too often we assume people know what our expectations are. Indeed, they rarely do. We have to communicate our needs and expectations clearly. How often we misinterpret someone's intention on the basis of an incorrect assumption about someone else's responsibility! Yet how easily this can be avoided through clear working agreements. Remember the dictum about the word "assume": It makes an ass out of u and me.

When I was a senior in high school, I worked as a cashier at a supermarket. After about a week, my responsibilities were increased to those of a clerk, a job I didn't want. After a day of denting cans that I dumped off a conveyor belt and taking four hours (instead of the normal one) to fill the vegetable trays with ice, I was called to the office. I protested that I signed up as a cashier, and this backbreaking labor wasn't my job. The manager then made me reread my employment agreement, which included the word "clerk" somewhere in the fine print. This was to include, besides the stacking of cans and bags of ice, a variety of other onerous jobs such as gathering shopping carts from the parking lot in the rain, loading garbage dumpsters, and maintaining the bathrooms. Being a passive-aggressive teenager, I completed these tasks with a combination of such sloth and incompetence, that I was soon back behind the cash register as a permanent cashier.

The importance of having a clear sense of your own position cannot be overemphasized. And it is equally important to have a clear sense of others' positions as well. Trust flourishes when personal and interpersonal barriers are diminished. In politically charged organizations, people tend to hide behind ambiguous roles and vaguely-worded or never-worded responsibilities. Clarifying relationships between workers, within groups, as well as between and among groups takes time and courage. With all working contracts, take the time necessary to ensure that all parties read all the print—fine and large. Revisit the understanding from time to time, especially those conditions you know to arouse confusion and misinterpretation. Periodically reviewing—and adjusting as necessary—one another's needs, expectations and role description is an excellent way to maintain trust.

Jane Maloney is an organizational development consultant reared on a combination of organizational development technology and psychodynamic interpretations of organizational behavior. Expertly aware of the multiple personal and interpersonal factors that will affect collaboration, she starts with role clarification and the charting of standards and responsibilities.

"Once you have agreement on your role and the role of others with whom you are working, then the personal and group dynamic trust issues and dilemmas can be seen more clearly for what they are. Sometimes I find that those interpersonal issues are solved by the role clarification itself."

Maloney's "responsibility charting" is one effective method of role clarification. This is a technique that involves all parties in identifying significant business activities and agreeing on what role each player has in the life cycle of each activity. Purchasing an expensive piece of equipment might be such an activity.

The joint responsibility charting procedure might give someone from senior management the role of being informed and ultimately responsible for authorization. Someone in middle management, say a department head, may need to be "cc'd." The supervisor overseeing the operation of this equipment may be the one who articulates the need, examines allocations, and specifies the equipment; and someone in accounting may simply cut the check. For these and other seemingly simple operations, lines of responsibility are often not well thought out, and necessary items get sandbagged by people who think they should have been consulted.

- ☐ How do you feel about this leader's perceptions of role confusion in the workplace and its possible elimination?
- ☐ With respect to your responsibilities, what roles among you and your associates are unclear?

Find an opportunity to review with one of your subordinates, a previously-implemented working arrangement.

Select one common major task in your organization that involves a few people. Interview each person to see how each perceives everyone's roles.

Risk Taking

All trust implies that a certain amount of risk and vulnerability exists between individuals. The word "trust" implies an equality between people that limits the fear of vulnerability: I trust you not to make me regret my openness with you. In most of our everyday interactions, even among intimates, however, this level of trust is rare. Most organizational climates encourage their members to "play it safe," that is, to avoid unconventional or risk-incurring behavior that might expose them to harm.

In organizations, harm usually comes from some form of punishment related to unwanted behavior. In some cases the definition of "unwanted behavior" in organizations is drawn so broadly that creative and innovative thinking is actively discouraged.

An employee's reluctance to come up with any innovative concepts can result from fear of betrayal. A colleague mistakenly perceived as an ally might plagiarize and claim credit for another's "good" ideas, or worse, that person might convey any "bad" ideas to others in an effort to discredit the originator.

"Can I trust you?" A colleague at a company I once worked for asked me. "What do you mean?" I asked. "Well, I'm so paranoid that whatever I say will get back to management. I'm sure at least one person is a spy, and I'm afraid I can't say anything to anyone without it going back." Well, I knew I wasn't a spy, and I knew what she was talking about because I had long ago decided to watch everything I said at this place. But suddenly I began to worry that she might be setting me up—a classic example of how the cycle of suspicion can negate the productive benefits that flow from an atmosphere where risk taking is nurtured and encouraged. After a brief checking-out period, we both took the risk and revealed our mutual disregard for the one we both suspected was the biggest rat anyway.

One way to encourage risk taking by others is to take risks yourself. Ask for feedback about specific actions you have taken. Prove to your people that there will be no danger in this. Build a team where the word is: "What a luxury! You can say almost anything to anybody here."

In an atmosphere where feedback is destructive, one is less likely to take risks. Conversely, a workplace where feedback is constructive and supportive encourages a willingness to take risks. This in turn helps build trust and confidence. You know you're in a trusting situation when you feel comfortable and at ease. You feel secure and accepted for who you are, and you don't feel that you have to prove yourself over and over again.

For trust to flourish, it helps to have an organizational culture that permits some error. As a supervisor, it is important to give people some "breathing room." Let them know that they do not need to ask your permission for every nonroutine decision. Allow them to find their own way. Once you have assessed a subordinate's level of task-related competence, give him or her the freedom appropriate under the given situation. Be willing to deal with differences of opinion in a patient and understanding way.

Michael Boyle directs the Creative Services Division at Foote Cone Belding/Leber Katz Partners, one of the largest Madison Avenue-type ad agencies. In response to a question related to one of my favorite mottoes, "Ask forgiveness, not permission," Boyle cautioned, "It depends on how creative and spontaneous the organization is and on how much credit you've accrued in your perception bank. I try to offer the kind of autonomy that gives lots of permission to begin with."

☐ How do you feel about this leader's perceptions of risk stifling in the workplace and its possible elimination?

> At an appropriate time, ask a supervisor, peer or subordinate for feedback about specific actions you have taken.

Mutuality and Sharing

Trusting relationships are reciprocal. A primary responsibility of any leader is to promote a sense of equality by shaping the behavior of others in the teamwork environment. Teamwork should be dictated by a sense of mutuality and sharing which discourages selfish behavior. This can best be accomplished by establishing jointly-determined procedures and systems. Team members will be happy to "play by the rules" which they themselves have created.

Thus, mutuality implies teamwork and reciprocity as well as taking responsibility, and I particularly like what Gerri Cevetillo has to say about being an active team player. Gerri is Vice President at Ultronics and Consumer Products Corporation, headquartered in Rockland County, New York. Having been in the business for over twenty years, she has seen a lot of changes in organizations and in the work-force.

"I recapture or gain trust by keeping my ego in check, being a team player, and not cheating the company or my coworkers. It seems to start with the ego. If you feel superior or entitled, you'll do things to erode others' trust in you. You'll start to bend the rules, ask for and take more than what you are allowed, and take shots at your fellow employees. I keep my ego in check by remembering that there is a lot of good talent out there, and I, just like everyone here, am not indispensable. I have to write a purchase order for paper clips just as everyone else must. It's the little things that add up to a mountain when you're dealing with the precarious nature of trust."

> ☐ How do you feel about this leader's perceptions of un-productive competition in the workplace and its possible elimination?

Task-Related Competence

Trust flourishes when reward and recognition are based on merit. Trust is eroded when promotions and status within the organization are based on politics rather than competence and achievement. Among the loudest cries of agreement I ever hear are the ones that come when I ask for a show of hands responding to the question, "Who here is now working for, or has in the past worked for, a clueless and incompetent supervisor?"

Now, you and I know that not *everyone* is so inept; the answer must lie within the trust factor. I believe perceptions of competence are related to perceptions of trustworthiness. You will be perceived as more competent if you share your motives for your behavior. Trust increases with increased understanding of why someone has chosen a course of action. Unknown motives combined with failure to inspire trust lead to limitless suspicion. In order to trust, one has to have faith in the other party's capability in performing the behavior which you are hoping for or expecting.

"Last man down, hatch secured!" Are the sacred words uttered just before a sub-marine dives…Nothing is more important than trust aboard a sub." Mark Mula, Director, Leadership and Management Development, for UBS, understands trust from a unique point of view, having been a U.S. Navy submarine officer. "The lessons I learned about trust aboard ship—faith in a sailor's 'intent' to keep his promise as well as his 'competency'—have been immeasurably useful in civilian corporate life. Strengthening the culture of trust is my unyielding personal and professional mission."

Most people answer in the affirmative when I ask, "Who here thinks that the Peter Principle applies: that organizations tend to promote people to their level of incompetence?" While such perceptions are influenced by dislike and distrust, upon probing, I discover some indisputable evidence: Supervisors and managers tend to want to be surrounded by people they like. Given a choice between like-ability and competence, it seems that these folks' competence gauge becomes rather lenient. To the degree that organizations accept this practice, employees will feel justifiable resentment towards management and, if not among the favorites, reflect proportional disloyalty.

Katalin Polgar, Ph.D., is a medical researcher who has worked in three countries, in each of which, the relationship of effort and merit to promotion is different: Hungary, Italy, and the United States.

"Having lived and worked in each of these countries, I have a good feel for the effect that favoritism has on productivity. Though never as politically repressive nor as passively compliant as the other so-called Communist bloc countries due to its strong Western alliances and blood-ties, Hungary was, nevertheless, Party-oriented, and your promotions in certain segments were dependent on being a Communist Party member in good standing. In Italy, family ties and personal relationships are so uniquely strong that promotions and other organizational relationships are shaped accordingly. Of the three, the U.S., as it advertises, is a land of opportunity relatively free of nepotism. It must be human nature, but here, too, in the U.S. there is some 'it's whom you know; not what you know,' but not anything like what I've known. Maybe that's why people here are so out-raged by favoritism. Whenever it occurs, people get angry and lose respect and trust. Such behaviors are both common and accepted in Europe in general. We may tease our American cousins, but I (and many other Europeans) respect Americans' relentless and quite often, non-hypocritical efforts in business and also their general ethics."

☐ How do you feel about these leaders' perceptions of de-structive politics in the workplace and its possible elimi-nation?

Interpersonal Sensitivity

Don't you hate it...When people call up and launch into their story/request/whatever, without once inquiring whether this is an OK moment for you. Or when people are so involved in themselves that you feel invisible around them—as if they could be talking to anyone, with no connection to anyone else's uniqueness. Or when people tell an off-color joke and are incapable of reading your expression of disgust, elbowing you to "get it" and laugh.

Interpersonal trust requires a sensitivity to feelings—your own and others'. No one will trust you if you don't show concern for them, their time, and their self-esteem. You can increase this interpersonal trust factor by simply inquiring about these concerns. "Would this be a good time to talk about that disagreement we were having?" and, "My intent in this conversation is to leave on a good note and to hear you out, not to punish you," are two excellent ways to reinforce trust.

Larry Tilley is a former superintendent of schools and college professor, and is currently an organizational development consultant and personal growth trainer. Larry has a lot to say about the word "trust" and its relationship to emotional maturity. Impressed by Goleman's work on Emotional Intelligence (EQ), he views EQ, like trust, as a function of personal awareness and interpersonal sensitivity. All of us who have worked with and studied under Dr. Tilley know his quip, "It takes two to know one." By this he means that a person must get feedback on the impact of his or her behavior on others. Only by seeing and understanding the impact of our words and behaviors on others and knowing where we stand with each other, can we modify these behaviors to continually improve our relationships.

☐ How do you feel about this leader's perceptions of insensitivity in the workplace and its possible elimination?

The Seven Conditions–Summing Up

Looking at the seven conditions of trust from an organizational perspective, the workplace should be seen as an environment where information is shared freely, where mutual expectations are discussed and agreements kept, where unnecessary micromanagement and controls are nonexistent, and where people are not afraid to tell the truth and "be themselves."

However, it is important not to overlook the dangers. Some people are unwilling to trust or are incapable of trusting behavior, and we must be on the alert to that

possibility. While I do take the position that trusting behavior begets trusting behavior and that in most circumstances, it's worth the risk of making that first
trusting move, there are exceptions.

Therefore what we have been discussing would be most appropriate in situations
where the "system" or organizational culture within which this interaction is taking place fosters trusting behavior rather than suspicious, gamelike behavior;
collaborative rather than competitive behaviors are rewarded; and there is a two-
way system of communication: supervisors, for example, get reviews from their
subordinates and they consider employee input before making decisions.

CHARACTERISTICS OF GREAT LEADERS

The Leader's Guide to Recapturing the Trust is a program for enhancing leadership.
The best way to examine the "look and feel" of trust and to establish a baseline
agreement of trust's place in leadership is to examine the following question: "In
thinking back to your most admired leader, mentor, coach, or supervisor, what do
you most remember about his or her style, behaviors, traits, or characteristics?

In worldwide surveys, the quality most often cited is "trustworthiness." Related
to this trust characteristic is an "interpersonal charisma." Variations of "visionary"
seem to come in second. "Vision" implies that the leader has a picture of where
the team or organization is going and what place his or her employees have in
that picture of what could be. "Coach" is cited next, representing a collection of
competencies including coaching and counseling delivered in a selfless, non-
judgmental way that promotes action without arousing defensiveness. Finally,
"business consultant" is cited. This leadership characteristic includes the concepts
of entrepreneur and change agent, adept at harnessing the knowledge and motivation of the work group and spearheading change. By confronting human and
business conflict and barriers, the "business consultant" achieves higher levels of
collaboration, inspiration, and productivity within the organization.

The four units in this book examine each of these essential characteristics in detail
and provide the tools and skills which will enhance your ability to be a leader who
thrives in this post-Enron landscape of public suspicion and mounting government regulation.

☐ What kinds of behaviors look "untrustworthy" to you?

☐ How about organizations in general? Think back to those whose products and/or services you have used over and over again. What might they have in common?

☐ What organizations might you consider working for? Investing in? Why?

THE YEARS OF DECLINING TRUST

Now that you have a better understanding of trust in the workplace today, let's take a look at how that environment has evolved. This historical perspective will help you more fully appreciate how trust has eroded in organizational life over the last half-century.

The Organizational Climate 1945–1960

World War II was finally over, and in the corporate world, American industry was white, male, and paternalistic. Rosie the Riveter returned home to bake and to care for her 2.2 kids, while dad took orders from some boss who had very likely been a military officer. In the decade after World War II, organizations were consciously structured like the military. Lines of command and communication, and conformity to rules were unquestioned. As long as they followed these organizational norms, employees had lifetime job security from a source they trusted as they would a brother or a platoon buddy.

This post-war generation grew up with certain expectations about life and work. Cautious and frugal, their parents believed in the value of hard work, and expected that their hard work and loyalty would be noticed and rewarded by a relatively benevolent organization, which would provide them, in exchange, with promotions, opportunities for feelings of belonging, and lifelong job security. To a large extent, until the 'eighties, this promise was kept. If you kept your nose clean, followed the rules, defended and hid behind your boss for protection, and came to work on time, you'd get the security, pension, and gold watch that you were working for. In business and at home, life was predictable and relatively peaceful.

Management training stressed understanding and reinforcing the rule books while, at the same time, reflective of the moral innocence of the time, management was also willing to examine the effect of human relations training.

The T-group a form of sensitivity training was inaugurated in 1947 by its founder, Kurt Lewin and a group of colleagues from MIT, and quickly became a popular leadership-training tool. Within a few years, thousands of people were to become involved in this training, and its approach was seen by most corporate officers as an excellent balance to an otherwise too-dominating military model of management.

But the T-group phenomenon was to last only a few years into the next decade. The attitudes that emerged from having attended a T-group were often at odds with the authoritarian leadership culture at the office. Work was still a long way from being a participatory democracy, where worker suggestions, let alone worker *feelings*, were solicited.

The Organizational Climate 1960–1980

The hippie era came to an end and the baby boomers had to go back to work. By the mid 'eighties, ex-members of the "youth culture" were climbing well into the managerial levels of American organizations. How ironic, after the dreams of the 'sixties, that this group would have to adjust to a work situation that required more hours, while offering relatively less pay and free time than their parents had enjoyed! America had begun to feel the effects of emerging global competition, and got shaken right down to its Calvinistic work-ethic roots. Hard times were to come. Management and organizational development training had to deliver programs related to quality and efficiency. Programs such as TQM (Total Quality Management) and other productivity and quality-training strategies were the rage of the 'eighties. These, coupled with dramatic advances in technology, led to significant increases in worker productivity and corporate profits.

As a result of corporate America's need to keep pace with its more productive and efficient foreign competitors, an era of downsizing emerged. At the same time, organizations squeezed what they could from the remaining workforce. Middle management all but disappeared, replaced by self-monitoring workteams, longer hours and higher standards for productivity and quality. The face of the American worker was now dour indeed. Trust levels began to seriously decline. Team-building efforts would attempt to restore morale but could not really manage the growing disappointment, fear and resentment.

The Organizational Climate 1980–TODAY

If the organizational structure looked like an hourglass in the mid 'eighties, it looked, according to Bob Jud, a change management thinker and practitioner, like "a Hershey bar with an almond in the middle of it." The flattened organizational schema is here to stay, it seems. Temporary project teams, not departments, dominate the organizational landscape.

And gone are the days when your boss took care of your future and your flanks. Gone are the days when you could put away your resume for a while after you landed a job. Gone are the days when you could keep a low profile and just do your own good work without having to publicize it throughout the organization.

Training programs in the 'nineties shifted to adapt to the service and information culture that America had become. During the 'nineties, our economic world hegemony depended upon our having cornered the "intellectual" markets, encompassing science, technology, medicine, and finance. Computer and software-design expertise was high on the list, followed by the various interpersonal communication skills.

Then with the turn of the century, misfortune and malfeasance overtook the organizational climate, and the mood in most public companies has turned grim. A lengthy recession has cut deeply into the prosperity we enjoyed in the 'nineties. The economy and the stock market are staggering under the weight of a politically and economically uncertain world, and continually emerging corporate scandals have deepened many stakeholders' distrust of American business. Rampant executive corruption and greed spawned by the absence of transparent, trustworthy corporate and financial leadership, have prompted a host of government regulations. Civil and criminal lawsuits abound. Corporate governance guidelines, mandated outside audits and compliance officers, codes of ethics and ethics training will soon be required by law. There is no question that the leadership skills so highly valued in the 'nineties are more important than ever in the new century. And underlying all of these skills is the ability to arouse and facilitate feelings of trust.

The Organizational Climate–Conclusion

The past half-century has seen changes in the business climate that have resulted in a crisis of trust. According to most surveys, working Americans over thirty see the past decade as the most stressful in their history, and there is little doubt that the stress will continue into the foreseeable future. We have lost the trust that enables the kind of feedback required to deal with interpersonal and organizational dilemmas, no less to confront unethical or illegal acts or intentions to act. Without trust, any efforts to legally mandate appropriate organizational conduct or create ethical dialog will fail.

THOUGHT QUESTIONS

Now, before moving on to Unit One, take a moment to ponder these questions:

⇨ Is the concept of "trust" important to you in general? Why?

⇨ How about at work?

⇨ Is yours a low-trust organization? How is this lack of trust displayed?

UNIT ONE

THE LEADER
AS AGENT OF TRUST

Being an agent of trust requires the ability to assess organizational trust at all levels and intervene on its behalf. In this unit you will be introduced to tools useful in assessing and maintaining trust. This involves: assessing how much you trust your coworkers, your supervisor and your organization; assessing your perception of the public's trust for the organization; and developing skills related to building trust throughout the organization.

These tools are essential in creating of an atmosphere that upholds and reinforces the ethics and transparency mandated by government regulators and supports the respectful confronting of potential breaches and ethical dilemmas throughout the organization.

Assessing Coworker Behaviors

Before we evaluate your supervisor and your organization with respect to trust, let's take a look at your perception of the trust behaviors of your coworkers. Respond to the questions on the facing page, regarding your experiences at your present workplace. Indicate if the identified actions occur: never or rarely (one point); sometimes (two points); often (three points); almost always (four points).

   ☐ Complete the scoring and compare your total to the
      norms below. How do your coworkers rate?

A score of above 28 points suggests that your coworkers create a rather low-trust work environment. If the score was between 14 and 28, you probably feel that, with respect to these issues, your coworkers create a comfortable environment.

   ☐ If you gave your coworkers a low rating, how optimistic
      are you about improvements?

COWORKER TRUST BEHAVIORS

In this organization, most people...

1   Don't express contrary opinions ⇨ _____

2   Intimidate or control others ⇨ _____

3   Take advantage of others ⇨ _____

4   Maintain hidden agendas ⇨ _____

5   Break commitments ⇨ _____

6   Are loose and vague about roles and responsibilities ⇨ _____

7   Don't offer timely feedback ⇨ _____

8   Divulge others' private personal data ⇨ _____

9   Conceal their personal vulnerabilities ⇨ _____

10 Plagiarize one another's ideas ⇨ _____

11 Communicate with destructive feedback ⇨ _____

12 Refuse to hear corrective feedback ⇨ _____

13 Treat others as numbers, not as valued partners ⇨ _____

14 Commit unethical or unprofessional acts ⇨ _____

TOTAL YOUR SCORE ⇨ _____

The Johari Window

An essential ingredient in the nurturing of trust is "authenticity." Simply put, authenticity is the respectful and supportive expression to another, when appropriate, of your personal reactions and feelings regarding that person's behavior in a specific instance or in general. This is the essence of giving and receiving feedback, which in the context of trust, consists of an honest exchange between people, describing how they perceive and are affected by each other's attitudes and behavior. Take a moment and give some thought to how you feel about this concept and then consider when authenticity might be useful.

One of the best ways to understand the connection between authenticity and trust is the Johari Window. Understanding the Johari Window leads to the essential skill of giving and receiving feedback. The Johari Window, named for its creators, Joseph Luft and Harry Ingram, is a model that shows the amount of openness existing between people in any social context.

The Johari Window is divided into four areas (See *Figure 1*). The *open* area consists of "things I know about me and others know about me;" the *blind* area consists of "things I don't know about me but others do know about me;" the *hidden* area consists of "things I know about me but others don't;" and finally, the *unknown* area includes the "things about myself which no one knows"

The result of giving and receiving feedback is to open the Johari Window, as in *Figure 2*, so that the *open* area becomes larger.

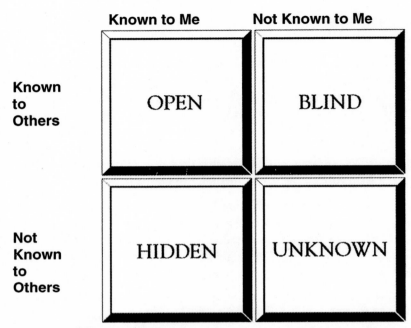

FIGURE 1–JOHARI WINDOW

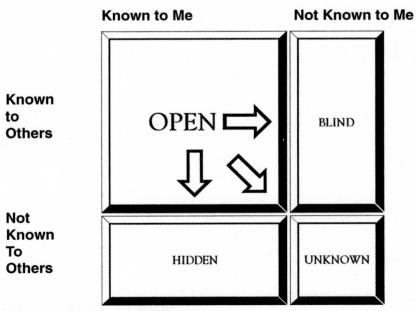

FIGURE 2–JOHARI WINDOW

We do this by diminishing the other areas: the more I tell you about my reactions, thoughts, and feelings towards you, the smaller my hidden area; the more you tell me about your reactions to me, the smaller my blind spot. This reduction of hidden and blind areas also reduces the unknown area. This surfacing of a host of aspects of yourself that were hidden in the previous more restricted Johari condition is a side benefit of such exposure.

By becoming more in touch with previously unknown aspects of yourself and responses to others, you can enhance your interpersonal skills in the workplace.

☐ Under what circumstances would you recommend that people "open up" their Johari Window? Are there circumstances under which you would not recommend this?

☐ Considering your responses to the trust assessments, how open would you say that people's Johari Windows are in your organization? If yours is a low-trust environment, how might "opening up" improve the situation?

Most people aren't aware of their personal reaction to others. When I ask people to describe their first impressions of, or reactions to, others whom they meet for the first time in one of my classes or workshops, few have distinct feelings that they can articulate. After a series of interpersonal and group classes, however, these same people are capable of sensing and expressing both their early and their subsequent emotional reactions toward one another's style/image and behavior. Once you become mindful of the interpersonal moment, you receive an array of significant visual and auditory cues: postures, vocal tones, grooming, and body language. Each of these cues can, in turn, trigger reactions in you to use as data to help you find appropriate ways of dealing with individuals. Pay attention to what you may be feeling or sensing. Reactions such as "confusion," "shock," "intimidation," "pressure to agree," or "boredom" are all data points to consider in the evolving interpersonal picture.

In this book, you will discover a variety of ways to enhance trust and interpersonal influence by opening your Johari Window. High trust is associated with the skill of giving feedback in such a way as to increase the likelihood that the listener can hear that feedback without becoming defensive. High trust is also associated with the skill of accepting feedback in such a way that you are perceived as being nondefensive, thus increasing the likelihood that the speaker will offer it. There is an "intent" and a "skill" implied here. The intent is the willingness to use feedback as information, free of judgment or agenda; and the skill is the timing, tone, and wording you use so as not to arouse defensiveness.

At this point, it would be important to evaluate four aspects of organizational trust. On a personal level, we'll consider your "interpersonal charisma." Then we'll examine three aspects of trust in the workplace: First, does your supervisor inspire trust? Next, what is the trust level within your organization? And finally, how does the public view your organization?

Interpersonal Charisma

One of the most important personality ingredients for fostering trusting relationships is an ability to become less self-absorbed and more focused on the person with whom you are communicating. I refer to this skill as "interpersonal charisma"—not that public quality we associate with celebrities, but the personal magic that makes a person feel important and visible in your presence. To better understand the definition of charisma, and assess your own "charismatic style," answer "mostly true" or "mostly false" to the ten items in the *Interpersonal Charisma Evaluation* on the facing page, which I have adapted from Doe Lang's *Charisma Quiz*.

☐ Complete the scoring and compare your total to the norms below. What do you need to change in order to enhance your charismatic bearing?

☐ What do you perceive as the relationship between interpersonal charisma and trust, as suggested by the items in the evaluation?

If you answered "mostly true" to all of the odd-numbered questions and "mostly false" to all of the even ones, you have a perfect score. If you responded appropriately to seven or more of the items, you would be considered interpersonally charismatic.

Items four and eight relate to the skill of listening attentively when it may be difficult to do so. When you find yourself in this situation, attempt to analyze why it's so hard to listen attentively to these people. Rather than yielding to the temptation of walking away, see what happens if you make a conscious effort to be an attentive listener.

INTERPERSONAL CHARISMA EVALUATION

		T	F
1	Friends come to me with their problems	☐	☐
2	I worry about the impression I'm making	☐	☐
3	I have the ability to put people at ease	☐	☐
4	I find it hard to get excited about many of the things that excite people I know	☐	☐
5	I find something I like about most people I meet	☐	☐
6	My mind wanders when people address me	☐	☐
7	In spite of occasional setbacks I generally appear to be in high spirits	☐	☐
8	I find that most people don't have much to say	☐	☐
9	Most of my colleagues would be shocked to discover that I have problems not unlike theirs	☐	☐
10	I have little patience for people who burden me with their problems	☐	☐

Assessing Your Supervisor

Let's take a look at how your supervisor rates when it comes to inspiring trust. Respond to the questions on the facing page as they relate to your experiences at your present workplace. Indicate if the identified actions occur: never or rarely (one point); sometimes (two points); often (three points); almost always (four points).

    ☐ Complete the scoring and compare your total to the norms below. How does your supervisor rate?

A score above 28 points would indicate that you are part of a rather low-trust work environment. If the score was between 14 and 28, you probably feel quite trusting of your supervisor and must feel that, with respect to these issues, you have a good situation.

    ☐ If you gave your supervisor a poor rating, how optimistic are you about improvements?

DOES MY SUPERVISOR INSPIRE TRUST?

1   I can't express contrary opinions or
    disagreements   ⇨ _____

2   I am intimidated or controlled   ⇨ _____

3   I am taken advantage of   ⇨ _____

4   I suspect hidden agendas   ⇨ _____

5   Commitments are not honored   ⇨ _____

6   Roles and responsibilities are vague   ⇨ _____

7   Misunderstandings build up due to
    a lack of timely feedback   ⇨ _____

8   Highly personal data has not been
    kept confidential   ⇨ _____

9   I withhold my personal vulnerabilities ⇨ _____

10 My supervisor has plagiarized my
    ideas   ⇨ _____

11 Feedback tends to be cutting and
    unproductive   ⇨ _____

12 I can't offer corrective feedback   ⇨ _____

13 I am a number, not a valued partner   ⇨ _____

14 I have witnessed unethical or unpro-
    fessional behavior   ⇨ _____

TOTAL YOUR SCORE   ⇨ _____

Assessing Your Organization

In order to evaluate how your organization rates when it comes to inspiring trust, answer "mostly true" or "mostly false" to the questions in the quiz on the following page, as they relate to your experiences in your present workplace.

☐ Complete the scoring and compare your results to the norms below. How does your organizational climate rate?

If your response to any of the questions was "mostly false," that item is probably a problem and bothers you and a lot of people in your organization. If more than three of your responses were "mostly false," you probably see supervision in your organization as untrustworthy and probably have a rather cynical view of life in the organization.

☐ If you gave your organization a poor rating, how optimistic are you about improvements?

THE TRUST LEVEL IN MY ORGANIZATION

		T	F
1	People can express their opinions	☐	☐
2	People can take risks and try creative strategies	☐	☐
3	Senior management is honest in spirit and behavior with its mission and value statements	☐	☐
4	Working agreements are clear	☐	☐
5	Performance reviews and evaluations are fair	☐	☐
6	Termination procedures are fair	☐	☐
7	Expectations are clear among departments	☐	☐
8	Effective interpersonal skills are valued and rewarded	☐	☐
9	Civility is valued	☐	☐
10	Differences are honored and diversity is seen as beneficial to the organization	☐	☐
11	Teamwork is valued	☐	☐
12	There are competitive and fair compensation and incentive programs	☐	☐
13	Promotions tend to be based on results	☐	☐
14	Management, from the senior level on down, listens to reactions, needs, and feelings from others, regardless of their position or status	☐	☐

Assessing the Public's Perception of Trust

And now take a moment to assess the public's perceptions of trust related to your organization. One way to do this is to consider how the various stakeholders may feel. Today, more than ever before, the perceptions of these stakeholders— prospective employees, customers, investors and regulators are critical for your organization's success. While you may not know the precise data, you probably can make a highly educated guess related to the questions in the quiz on the facing page. Use a trust scale of 1 to 5 (lowest to highest perceptions of trust).

☐ Complete the scoring and compare your results to the norms below. How does your organization rate?

A score of 3 or below suggests that the public takes a rather skeptical view of your organization. If the score was 4 or 5, you probably feel that the public holds your organization in high esteem.

☐ If you gave your organization a poor rating, how optimistic are you about improvements?

It has been shown that there is a very high correlation between the public's trust for an organization and the trust levels existing within that organization. For this and other reasons outlined earlier, everyone in the organization must be an agent of trust helping to establish, maintain and recapture the trust, which can be so fragile in these challenging times.

THE PUBLIC'S PERCEPTION OF MY ORGANIZATION

1   Your public's perception of the
    integrity of your organization   ⇨ _____

2   Your organization's reputation
    among prospective employees   ⇨ _____

3   Your customers' trust in your
    product(s) and/or services   ⇨ _____

4   Your investors' trust in your stock   ⇨ _____

5   Your regulators' trust in your
    compliance to standards   ⇨ _____

TOTAL YOUR SCORE   ⇨ _____

CONCLUSION

You have now completed the first of the four units in this trust and leadership program. As an agent of trust, you have additional understanding of the position that trust has in American business today. You have examined the business-financial, social, and personal implications of low trust and have been exposed to the multiple ways in which trust can be defined and measured. The remaining three units are designed to strengthen those personal and leadership skills that will make you a leader who possesses the most respected characteristics identified earlier in this unit.

UNIT TWO

THE LEADER
AS COACH

You are about to address those areas that you discovered were lacking when you made your assessments in *Unit One*. You will be introduced to a number of concepts and skills associated with strong leadership so that you can be a coach—continuously monitoring and maintaining a trusting and productive environment. The skills include: Effective interpersonal communications; giving and receiving feedback; as well as one-on-one coaching and counseling. Return to any of these anytime you feel you need a refresher.

THE FUNDAMENTAL SKILLS FOR EFFECTIVE INTERPERSONAL COMMUNICATIONS

In order to be an effective and powerful leader it is necessary to build trust within the organization by shaping the trust and behavior of the people you supervise and work with. This means becoming a "people developer," with in-depth knowledge of these people's concerns, feelings, and attitudes. You can only achieve this understanding by acquiring strong interpersonal communication skills.

Active Listening

Too often we communicate poorly because we simply do not "hear" what the other person is saying. Our minds wander, we become distracted. Or we are framing our response before the other has even finished his statement. We need to make a conscious effort to *actively listen*. This is the skill of accurately perceiving the content and emotional tone of what we are hearing and then summarizing (or *paraphrasing*) for the speaker, our understanding of what he or she has expressed.

Paraphrasing can be as simple as a short restatement of fact, and might be expressed either as a question or in the declarative. You might begin your response with: "Then, are you saying…" or "In other words, you mean…" or "So you think that…" Sometimes, paraphrasing may involve explaining your perception of the other's feelings, or asking for a clarification of those feelings. In this case, you might preface your remarks with "You seem to feel that…" or "I gather that you are angry about…"

This technique can help communication in several significant ways. It slows the communication process, offering more time to think, feel, and reflect. It helps clarify the content and emotional background of what is being discussed. It raises the other's self-esteem by demonstrating an interest in what that person is saying. It can help dissipate the intensity of the other's emotional state, by indicating your understanding (though not necessarily your approval). And the feedback you provide helps the other clarify his or her own thinking.

> Apply this communication skill at the next appropriate opportunity. Ask, and find out if, indeed, your summary matches the other's intended meaning

Describing and Confirming Behavior

In any interpersonal communication situation, we are receiving and responding to two forms of communication: verbal and nonverbal. As we have seen, verbal communication can convey content and emotion, and needs to be clearly understood by both parties for trust to exist. Nonverbal communication—tone of voice, gestures, posture and other physical phenomena can also be indicators of another's intent and emotional state. This is true not only of conversation. A person's general deportment sends similar messages. The danger lies in our misreading these important signals.

A significant adjunct to active listening is the skill of describing and confirming these nonverbal signs, with the emphasis on *observing* and *identifying* performance or behavior without attempting to *interpret* the reasons for that behavior. More often than not, to do otherwise leads to erroneous conclusions, and a cycle of defensiveness ensues.

Defensiveness is a barrier to trust. We become defensive when we feel we are being threatened or attacked. At such times, we tend to stop listening to the other's message and start considering how we may counter the threat. Our defensiveness creates, in turn, defensiveness in the other individual, and the dialog, if unchecked, becomes increasingly destructive. Consider the following four situations. And keep in mind that people sometimes send nonverbal messages unconsciously with no awareness that they are doing it:

⇨ During a discussion of policy and procedures with a fellow team member, you notice that the tone of his voice is different than usual. Is he expressing anger? Impatience with your ideas? Or is this how he expresses enthusiasm and excitement?

⇨ While interviewing a candidate for promotion, you notice that she is trembling. Do you inspire fear? Is she nervous?—in which case, she might be unqualified for the position. Or is the thermostat on the air conditioner set too low?

⇨ The person you are conversing with repeatedly shakes his finger at you. Is he threatening you? Trying to intimidate you? Being accusatory? Or might he just use this gesture to emphasize what's important to him?

⇨ An employee to whom you have assigned a task is performing in an uncharacteristically slow way. Is this an indication of dissatisfaction or resentment? A sign of insubordination? Or did the baby keep her up 'til three in the morning, yet she dutifully made the 6:20 train so she would not be late for work?

What is the correct course of action in any of these situations (or countless others like them)? How do you stop the cycle of defensiveness before it starts? Ask!

In a constructive and supportive way, point out that aspect of the other's behavior that bothers you and, when appropriate, explain how it affects you. The answer you get may surprise you! And you may find that you get to know the person a little better.

> Apply this communication skill at the next appropriate opportunity. Compare what you discover to what you might have assumed about the other person's intent.

Managing Feelings or Personal Reactions

We have learned that one important component of *active listening* is focusing on the feelings that others express. One of the biggest challenges in interpersonal communication is how to deal with others' feelings. And we can only meet that challenge if we are capable of dealing with our own. Feelings are an indicator of our comfort level with ourselves, with others, and with our ideas; not dealing with them can be a source of considerable conflict among people.

To build trust through interpersonal sensitivity, you must be in touch with your own feelings and attuned to the feelings of others. The more in touch you are with your feelings about someone or something, the clearer you will be about what action you should or should not take. And the more you are aware of the feelings of others, the better you will be able to communicate. The skillful expression of your feelings can create an open, supportive climate. When confronted with strong feelings (like those you experience when you are in conflict with someone), take time to examine them. Also, give words to those feelings in order to communicate them to yourself and the other person. When you feel anger, pain, fear, love, or joy about some specific event, place, person, or idea, say so.

Managing feelings is the skill of delivering your personal reaction calmly and supportively without arousing emotions and defensiveness, by transforming blaming statements into descriptions of feelings. Statements like "You're irresponsible," or "What you did was so dumb," while they may *demonstrate* your feelings, do not *communicate* them in a productive way. They create distance and trigger the other person's defensiveness.

To effectively apply defense-reducing communication and constructively convey to someone how his or her behavior has affected your feelings, you might use a statement like: "I'm angry with you for missing that appointment..." or "I'm disappointed in you for going back on your promise..." or "Your statement about my productivity really bothered me, and it's been upsetting me all day..."

The free expression of feelings is important for physical, psychological, and inter-personal reasons. When anger is denied, for example, it turns inward and usually emerges as depression, hostility, or some other undesirable emotion. Respect, accept, and express your feelings. If you can accept your feelings, you can accept yourself. If you can accept yourself, you can accept others. Addressing feelings in this way will sustain the best of relationships and encourage the development of new ones.

> Apply this communication skill at the next appropriate opportunity. Compare its effectiveness to that of other less interpersonally-sensitive approaches.

APPLYING THE FUNDAMENTAL COMMUNICATION SKILLS

The interpersonal communication skills you have learned can be used to build trust in your organization. In this section, we will explore some of the ways you can put these skills to work using the feedback process. We will examine how the process works in a number of situations, including: confronting performance problems, asking for feedback from a defensive supervisor, and dealing with an attitude or performance concern with a peer or subordinate.

Confronting Performance Problems

Feedback, be it positive or negative, when honestly exchanged between and among people, is the foundation of the seven conditions of trust. Being open to giving and receiving feedback about the helpful and the non-helpful things we say and do is the ultimate interpersonal communication skill, and it draws upon all of the others: interpersonal charisma, active listening, describing and confirm-ing behavior, and managing feelings.

Our behavior sends messages to those around us. When someone shares with us their reactions to our messages, they are giving us feedback. Sharing feedback can help us understand each other's behavior, feelings, and motivations; our *interpersonal charisma* is the primary facilitator.

Finger pointing and judgmental statements are not feedback. They are the means to getting even and hurting others. They do not build trust, and they have no place in interpersonal communications. You may find that, as a result of the widespread use of these devices, many people will be reluctant to expose themselves to constructive, helpful feedback.

In order to deliver feedback effectively, use the interpersonal techniques that were presented earlier in this unit.

Manage your feelings. The offering of feedback must be done in a caring, supportive way, free of acrimony, and should refer to something that can be changed in the individual receiving it. Let him or her know you are interested in improving your relationship.

Feedback should be given in private (or among other supportive people), preferably soon after the triggering event, so the details can be reasonably well remembered. There must be clear indications that the listener is ready to receive feedback. If not, the message either won't be heard or will be misinterpreted.

Describe and confirm the receiver's behavior: Report exactly what took place, withholding your ideas as to why things happened or what was meant by them. Actively listen as you let the receiver of the feedback describe what the behavior means or as you explore its meaning together. Using your interpersonal communication skills can be equally effective in receiving feedback from others. Graciously guide them through the process of active listening, describing and confirming behavior, and managing feelings.

It is also important to respect the right of the receiver to possibly disagree with your feedback. The receiver may see things differently from you. Be willing to hear his or her response. This can lead to a dialog that will ultimately resolve the conflict. We will further explore the concepts of conflict mediation later in this unit, but first let's consider some of the other practical applications of giving and receiving feedback.

Asking for Feedback from a Defensive Supervisor

When you are in disagreement with, unsure where you stand with, or feeling distrustful or alienated towards your supervisor, asking for feedback can be the most effective means to recapture the trust. Be careful, though; confronting a defensive or manipulative superior has its hazards. To accomplish this, the most frequently requested of all business skills, I recommend the following action steps, adapted from those designed by Dr. Bernard Rosenbaum, while he was serving as President of MOHR Development, Inc.

⇨ Determine a mutually convenient time to discuss a business, professional, or personal matter.

⇨ Start by allowing this person an "out." Avoid having him or her feel "cornered," that is, required to give you feedback. Say something like, "Maybe it's in my head, J.B., but lately I've noticed…" This statement will allow your superior an opportunity to get off the hook by saying, "Yeah, it's all in your head, now scram."

⇨ The point here is to alert this individual to your concern. Whether he or she wishes to acknowledge the issue at the moment is less important than the fact that the concern has been raised and will have an impact on your relationship. This may be as far as you can go.

⇨ While maintaining sensitivity to your supervisor's position and concerns, indicate that you can "take the heat" by getting to the point with specifics. Introduce your specifics by saying something like, "It's important that I fully understand and respond to your needs and expectations, so please let me know where I seem to be off-base. There are a couple of signs that tell me I've been missing something."

⇨ In a non-accusatory way, indicate wherein your perception or views of the problem situation differ from your supervisor's. While it is essential that your presentation be made with confidence, the respect with which you deliver your presentation is equally important.

⇨ After identifying your supervisor's behaviors and how you have interpreted them, check the validity of your perceptions and listen non-defensively to whatever reactions evolve.

⇨ If confused about the specific behaviors and/or performance that may have aroused those perceptions, respectfully ask for specific instances, so that you may better work at changing these behaviors, should that be indicated.

⇨ Since misconceptions, disconnects and the like generally result from a combination of both parties' behaviors, it could therefore be useful if you were to discuss with your supervisor, those things that might be said or done to improve your relationship. Identify those behaviors that he or she might adopt to help you modify your performance.

⇨ Thank this person for the feedback, letting him or her know what you will do, by when, and how both of you will be able to recognize the value of this conversation. That—confronting your superior—is perhaps the most difficult of the touchy organizational communications techniques.

    ☐ How do you feel about these steps?

    ☐ Would these steps work for you? If not, how might you modify them?

Dealing with an Attitude or Performance Concern with a Peer or Subordinate

Now let's turn to the second most frequently requested skill: dealing with working relationships at an equal level or with subordinates. These relationships involve a different set of risks and obstacles. To be successful in the workplace, you need to keep peers as allies as much as possible, and you need to maintain the loyalty, morale, and motivation of your staff.

Disappointments and disconnects are happening all the time at work. The sooner you approach these situations in a constructive way, the more trust you can build and maintain. In most situations, adapting the following strategy to your particular style and interpersonal performance structure will elicit a favorable response from peers and subordinates.

⇨ Determine a mutually convenient time to discuss a business, professional, or personal matter.

⇨ At the meeting, indicate your intent, your ultimate objective for the meeting; it should be to repair some misunderstanding or error, so that the air can be cleared and your working (or personal) relationship put back to "normal."

⇨ Focus on the specific behavior. It might be, for example, a performance problem, a job skill deficiency, an inappropriate statement, or an unethical act. Indicate why you consider it a matter of concern. Make it clear that you would like to hear your peer or subordinate's side of the issue and discuss it.

⇨ Actively listen to his or her response, demonstrating your goodwill in hearing the reasons and letting the individual fully respond and feel "heard."

⇨ Action step five: Reasonably soon, focus on the "future" and what you both can do, so that the situation will improve.

⇨ Write down and commit to those promises made by both of you, so that this and other similar events are less likely to occur in the future.

⇨ Indicate your confidence in this individual's ability to honor these commitments. Set a follow-up date to note progress and/or completion.

☐ How do you feel about these steps?

☐ Would these steps work for you? If not, how might you modify them?

One-on-One Coaching and Counseling

One-on-One Coaching and Counseling is an important role of the leader in a trusting environment. Like giving feedback, to which it is intimately related, serving as professional advisor requires applying the interpersonal communication skills.

Counseling is commonly (and erroneously) perceived as telling or showing someone how to do something or as giving advice. Many supervisors tend to listen to an employee's problem and offer a solution. While this saves time, it denies the leader an opportunity to mentor and develop the subordinate. A far more effective "helping " technique is to assist others to help themselves. That means listening to them, asking questions, and assisting them in identifying and selecting possible solutions, thereby encouraging independence and self-reliance.

Be an interviewer. The capability to define the problem and identify its solution is usually within the person who needs the help. By asking questions and actively listening, you can help someone accurately state the problem and find the answer. This technique of helping others help themselves fosters self-esteem and confidence, leading to greater self-reliance and, ultimately, to higher productivity.

CONCLUSION

Interpersonal communication is a mechanism by which people send and receive verbal and nonverbal messages. On a deeper level, it is a very important process by which people have a chance to uncover and discover themselves and others. In Unit Two, you have examined the fundamental skills of interpersonal communications essential to the trust-building feedback process and learned some additional ways to supportively encounter, coach, and counsel others in order to improve relationships and performance throughout the organization. Disciplined use of the communication skills will give you the necessary "interpersonal charisma" to deal with even the most difficult of business relationships.

UNIT THREE

THE LEADER
AS BUSINESS CONSULTANT

The leader as business consultant has a very sophisticated view of professional management. This coveted skill takes the skills of coaching and counseling individuals and converts them into group, intergroup and organization-wide analysis and consultation. With the skills in this unit, you will become a business consultant to your unit and organization by helping your people respond to continuous changes in the business climate and the marketplace.

You'll be introduced to a set of tools and techniques in each of three areas vital to organizational change and development: the force-field analysis, team leadership, and conflict mediation. *The force-field analysis* is a step-by-step technique that facilitates group problem solving and action planning. It empowers those employees who are involved in a challenging situation to assess and manage that problem by developing a detailed and self-monitoring action plan. It is the premier tool for responding to continuous organizational change and renewal. *The team leadership skills* will provide a series of group and inter-group activities to establish teamwork, stimulate morale and manage group conflict through collaboration. *The conflict mediation action steps* will help you manage differences and reach win-win understandings between yourself and others, between two others, and between groups.

FACILITATING GROUP PROBLEM-SOLVING

The Force-Field Analysis

The concept of the force-field analysis is based on the understanding that all organizational phenomena—such as "the level of morale" or "the amount of profit generated"—are determined by "forces" in people and in the overall "system." Among these forces are management, policies, the marketplace, and the competition.

The force-field analysis is an instrument that helps visualize these forces. A wavy line in the middle represents the current state or situation; a goal statement on the upper right represents the desired end point; and a series of arrows pointing toward and away from the goal meeting at the "current situation" line represent driving and restraining forces. The process calls for the adding on to the number or strength of the driving forces and the taking away from the number or strength of the restraining forces so as to move that wavy "current situation" line closer to the goal.

Using the model on a chart board in front of a group, apply the following action steps to facilitate the Force-Field Analysis:

⇨ Have the group generate a list of relevant issues, challenges and needs that should be addressed.

⇨ Have the group select the one issue that feels most immediate and significant.

⇨ Convert that issue into a positive goal statement that will be a motivating reach. For example, an issue of poor morale can have a goal statement of "high morale."

⇨ Have group members work individually to identify driving forces and restraining forces. Driving forces are already existing forces that are encouraging "high morale." Restraining forces are the existing forces that are interfering with "high morale." Indicate that most forces exist in the "system" and in the people involved.

⇨ Chart the forces reported by the group members

⇨ Help the group critique and evaluate each of the forces, prioritizing them in order of feasibility and practicality.

⇨ Start with one force, generally a restraining force. A helpful analogy can be found in the sales axiom: "The undermining of an objection is the quickest way to the sale." The objection is the force; how to remove or overcome the objection is the action plan; and the sale is, of course, the goal. Facilitate a self-monitored action plan where each participant takes an active role in identifying the *who, what,* and *when.*

Direct your work-team in a problem-solving session concerning an issue at work. Start with the question of what your team would like as a high-reaching goal. Then follow the guidelines to discover the variety of driving and restraining forces. Lead the group into an action plan of shared responsibilities and accountability.

TEAM LEADERSHIP

Just as you have developed trust with and among your coworkers and employees, you can build trust within teams.

Trust-Building for Teams

The concept of team playing is very American. It suggests a fairness where all players play by common rules and are punished by common penalties. Too often, teams have gotten a bad rap in organizations because, for political reasons, some people are able to play by different rules. Nobody likes favoritism. It erodes trust and breaks down the potentially great benefits of teamwork. Team building is all about trust. Once trust is attained within a group, no one counts who has done more than whom. Teamwork suggests a belief in the synergy of the group: that more productivity, more creativity, more profit, more of anything we individuals want, will result from doing something together rather than doing it alone.

The best way to cultivate and reinforce trust and teamwork is to have the group "process" its relationships. Process, in this context means to "discuss the underlying relationship issues." Certain underlying relationship issues need to be presented to team members so that they may critique and evaluate the behaviors exhibited by the team, as well as the group's progress. This can be accomplished by having team members respond, using a scale of 1 to 10 (low to high), to the following *team assessment questionnaire*:

⇨ Was the session conducted in a spirit of trust and openness?

⇨ Did participants demonstrate listening skills and empathy?

⇨ Were all relevant players involved and did they participate?

⇨ Were differences respected?

⇨ Were roles and responsibilities clearly understood?

⇨ Did Individuals feel a sense of belonging?

It's best to ask these questions after some team task, limiting the participants' responses to reactions about only their teamwork during this last task.

> Have your group or team spend up to one hour on any of its routine tasks. Afterwards, making sure the members focus only on the previous hour, have them assess the quality of their teamwork by responding to the "team assessment questionnaire."

You may notice that, by simply comparing your scores, you are building trust and openness. Keeping the feedback to the immediate past situation limits unproductive blaming and the bringing up of hurtful unresolved past conflicts. Care should be taken to keep the discussion focused on the specific issues related to the preceding group task. As the facilitator of the group, you may neither choose, nor need to, examine the feelings or issues behind the scores. Sometimes, the data is enough and things are better left unsaid.

However, should there be some conflict worth examining, you may choose to speak about the issues beyond the instrument's simple acknowledgement. But this decision must be made only after considering the willingness and ability of the group (or affected individuals) to confront and manage conflict.

The Strength Bombardment

Another team-building tool is the *strength bombardment*, sometimes called a "validation exercise." It is an experience that leaves everyone buoyant and optimistic. It, like all human relations training, reinforces trust through authentic contact, self-disclosure, the clarifying of roles and expectations, the fostering of equality, and the suspension of the impersonal attitudes and behaviors that arise from status differences.

Here's how it works: In a group of three to no more than eight individuals, have each person think about each of the people in the group. These people may know one another for some time or not, just as long as they have had some exposure to one another, enough to have gathered some "first impression" intuitive data.

Have each in turn be on the "spot"—a happy spot, that is, because each of their counterparts will, one at a time, identify some specific thing he or she likes about the person: one thing that the person said or did that may have been enjoyed, appreciated or identified with and caused a good feeling about the person.

This technique can be used even among people who may be angry with or mistrustful of one another. The point is not to fake a liking, but rather to set aside, if necessary, any negative thoughts and enjoy that component of the other's behavior that is liked. The effect on group morale and individual joy is remarkable!

CONFLICT MEDIATION

There will be situations when the mutual giving and receiving of feedback or the coaching and counseling process will be insufficient to "clear the air," especially in heated disputes between you and a coworker or between two of your subordinates. If, under these circumstances, the interpersonal communication skills we have discussed thus far seem inadequate, they may be augmented by conflict management techniques. We will explore these techniques as they relate to two specific situations: the first, a conflict between you and one other person, in which you will employ *do-it-yourself mediation*; the second, a conflict between two others, which requires you to provide *third-party mediation*. For a more detailed description of these techniques, you may wish to refer to work of Dan Dana at www.mediationworks.com, upon which the following discussion is based.

Do-It-Yourself Mediation

This method of resolving a conflict between you and one other involves the following action steps:

⇨ Find a time to talk: Approach the other person, identifying the issue and ask him or her to join you in a conversation. Agree upon a time and place and ensure an understanding that you will both stay until you have reached mutual agreement that the discussion is over, and that neither of you will use intimidation or force a one-sided solution.

⇨ Plan the context: Make sure there will be sufficient time for the meeting and that there will be no interruptions, and do what is necessary to provide privacy and other comforts.

⇨ Talk it out: Enter into a dialog that enables a full description of both sides of the situation. The objective is to reach the *breakthrough*, when you and the other person will shift from "me against you" fighting to an "us against the problem" search for solutions. This requires that you perform two tasks: the first is continuous discussion about the issues in disagreement for as long as necessary to reach the breakthrough; the second is acknowledgement of conciliatory gestures made by the other person, and offering them yourself when you can do so sincerely.

⇨ Finalize the deal: The important features of most successful agreements are: first, they are perceived to be balanced. They feel like "you win, I win" situations, where both parties benefit, and sacrifices or compromises are shared; in addition, they are behaviorally specific, in that they define what each party will do or say in the future; and finally, they are in writing.

Third Party Mediation

Resolving conflict between two others can be accomplished using the following action steps:

⇨ Decide whether to mediate: Mediation is appropriate in conflicts between two people of relatively equal status. On the other hand, there are some nonmediatable issues, such as illegal or unethical behavior or lack of job skills, which might be better suited to resolution by some other method or authority.

⇨ Hold preliminary meetings: Prepare both parties by defining the problem, establishing your neutrality, and obtaining both parties' commitment to the mediation process.

⇨ Plan the context: Make certain that there will be sufficient time for the meeting and do what is necessary to provide privacy and other comforts, while protecting the meeting from interruptions, walkouts, or power plays.

⇨ Hold the three-way meeting: As with do-it-yourself mediation, the objective is to reach the *breakthrough*. This is best accomplished by three means: first, maintaining the "essential process," that is, encouraging continuous discussion and preventing withdrawal; second, supporting conciliatory gestures; and third, remaining neutral and patient.

⇨ Finalize the deal: Facilitate the deal so that it is balanced, behaviorally specific and confirmed in writing.

⇨ Support the deal: Provide reinforcement through regularly scheduled follow-up meetings.

Managing Conflict between Groups

A final method of conflict mediation, and very effective trust-building tool is the *group-on-group encounter model*. This works well in situations where hostile and untrusting behaviors have gone on for some time. In this classic model, designed by Richard Beckhart, two opposing units (two classically mistrusting departments, for example) go to an offsite. A facilitator gives each group three blank sheets of newsprint, one entitled "what we think of us," the second, "what we think of them," and the third, "what we think they think of us." Encouraging each group to write its perceptions down in this way helps to reduce possible awkward timidity.

It is astounding how little of this direct feedback occurs in organizations. In all my years of conducting this, the most poignant of trust-building exercises, I've never seen negative fallout, either immediate or long-term. One caution, however: the qualified professional facilitator should know the culture, departments, and individuals sufficiently well to determine the boundaries of acceptable responses and the appropriate circumstances for timely interventions.

CONCLUSION

The fundamental skills for effective interpersonal communication can be used to promote understanding and trust among people. A leader with business consulting skills possess a rare gift: the ability to facilitate conflict resolution, group problem diagnosis and planning, as well as team and interteam collaboration. The skills you have acquired in Unit III will enable you to act as a "change agent," helping your organization respond to the continuously evolving demands in the marketplace.

UNIT FOUR

THE LEADER
AS VISIONARY

The hallmark of a visionary leader is the ability to evaluate his or her people and inspire them with insight and enthusiasm about how their competencies can play an essential role in the organization's future. Most people are unaware of the powerful forces inside of them and in their environments that shape their "personality": their wants, values, goals and competencies. The more aware you are of these factors, the better leader you will become: more consistent and authentic.

When you have completed this unit, you will better understand the concepts of *image and identity* and *professional competencies*. Once know yours, you will be in a position to better help your people gain the personal satisfaction of knowing theirs. You will also be able to guide them with respect to which of their personal attributes should be surfaced and "mixed and matched" to better fit the needs of the organization.

So, let's take a look at who *you* are. We'll examine the forces that have shaped your role choices, and, relevant to this program's objective, we'll explore what you need to do to be a more skillful agent of trust and a visionary leader.

We'll begin this unit with an exploration of your *self-concept*. These exercises are essential to clarifying the self-concept and are central to the process of building visionary leaders.

SELF-CONCEPT

Your self-concept is made up of your values, competencies, personal style, life history and goals. Put them all together in a systematic cohesive way, and your choices of roles and responsibilities in life and work will become clearer and more satisfying. The exercises that follow require a high degree of self-awareness. Some of this awareness can be achieved through quiet reflection and introspection; some needs to be provided by the feedback of trusted others.

These exercises are the foundation of career counseling, a skill possessed by all great leaders. Only those who themselves go through a self-concept review can skillfully lead others through the same process.

Work Values

Think back to a moment in your work life when you felt great! It may have been early in your life or more recent, but be sure it was work-related, not play-related, even if there was no financial compensation involved. Who was there? What made it so enjoyable?

What does this event say about what's most meaningful to you in work situations? What was it about the working environment, the people involved, how were you treated?

Which common elements emerge? What conclusions might you draw about what motivates you and most others at work? Would it be *recognition, achievement, challenge,* or perhaps *the nature of the work itself?*

☐ What can you do to make the people you supervise feel
   that they are having a "peak work experience"?

You may want to reflect upon how the principles embodied in the *seven conditions of trust* and the skills inherent in *effective interpersonal communication* could have played a part in creating your peak work experience.

> The next time you are conducting a job interview or
> performance review session, ask about past highly
> satisfying work moments and discuss the insights and
> implications. You can gather a great deal of critical
> information from the response!

Competency Review

Everyone should be doing things that they not only like, but are good at.

> Think of the success experiences of your life. Write them down. From this recall, you'll be able to generate a list of your best talents, skills, and abilities…those that should be part of your everyday working life.

LIFE HISTORY RETROSPECTIVE

The word "trust" produces strong reactions in most people. Each individual sees the concept differently, and will interpret its meaning differently, even as it applies to the same moment or event. In my book, *Recapturing the Trust*, I included a chapter on my personal history, outlining some significant moments which profoundly affected and enhanced my appreciation for and fascination with trust: forces that shaped my perceptions regarding the condition of trust and my view of the factors that have impacted trust in American institutions.

Just as I examined my life history and isolated some key experiences to gather insights into the meaning and significance of trust in my life, you can do the same: Reflect on parallel moments of your own and think about how these moments have affected your feelings about trust and confidence in others and in the institutions in which you have worked and lived.

GOALS AND GOAL-SETTING

The last component of the self-concept consists of your life/work goals. With some reflection on your life's highs and lows, and armed with some thinking about your competencies and work values, you should be able to articulate a challenging work goal that will satisfy you personally and professionally.

Envision current opportunities and/or those likely to emerge in the near future, and identify a challenging goal.

Project at least a few months into the future and identify a specific set of tasks or roles related to that goal.

Write your goal on a piece of paper. Pause for a moment to reflect. Then repeat the process several times. The positive or negative thoughts that spring into your mind are your beliefs about your chances for accomplishing the goal.

What are your thoughts telling you about your chances for success or failure? If they say "Go for it!" make your decision public and get support from others in setting milestones and target dates for achieving your goal. If your mind is resisting, take a long lingering look at what the barriers are and take steps to overcome those barriers or modify the goal. You are now ready to create a detailed action plan, complete with the "who, what and when" of your well-formulated goal.

Now that you've clarified your own self-concept and examined your work goal, you have the tools to help your people explore and discover their own self-concepts. Lead them through the same exercises that you have just completed. The ability to help people reinvent themselves at work in this way—motivating and encouraging them towards fulfillment of their potential for the organization, and providing the spark that makes it all possible—is the defining attribute of a visionary leader.

CONCLUSION

I'm sure this final unit has been a very personal journey for you. You have gained an intimate familiarity with those factors that have shaped your personal-and work-image identities—your values, talents, hopes and goals, and life-defining events: factors that are essential to great leadership. Your authentic response to the subtle and changing moods, needs, and motivations of others is closely linked to your response to these very things within yourself. This human connection, this empathy might, in fact, be the most essential of all the tools for establishing, maintaining and/or recapturing the trust.

IN CONCLUSION

Having completed *The Leader's Guide to Recapturing the Trust*, you have learned, practiced, and applied the many models, instruments, action steps, skills and leadership techniques that will enable you to inspire trust at every level within your organization and earn the confidence of your organization's every stakeholder. As a result of your efforts, you will be gathering professional and emotional dividends continuously…and, so will everyone with whom you interact!

Although this milestone marks the completion of a significant task, it is really a beginning.

While the concepts and skills you have acquired are simple, they are not easy to retain. You may find yourself tempted not to practice them, or forget how. It's easy to fall into old habits, especially in these troubling times when it seems as though you're the only one who seems to care and everyone is looking out for his or her own self-interest.

You may therefore wish to augment what you have learned.

My commitment is to stay in touch with you and to provide a contact source for questions and discussion. Visit my website at www.recapturingthetrust.com to learn about opportunities for further skill development:

⇨ Trust audit

⇨ Management/organizational consultations

⇨ Online training

⇨ Other training resources

⇨ *Management strategy and feedback seminars* and

Face-to-face communications laboratories sponsored

by The Institute for Business Development

Management strategy and feedback seminars and *face-to-face communications laboratories* are leadership training vehicles that can help sharpen your interpersonal skills.

I was introduced to this training by Dr. Larry Tilley, who since the mid-nineteen-sixties, has introduced thousands of individuals to the art of sensitivity training. The face-to-face communications laboratory is based on the principles and techniques of the "human relations training group," or "hrt," commonly referred to as the "T-Group," which originated in the late nineteen-forties.

Initially, the T-group was designed for and delivered to high-level leaders to sharpen their ability to give and receive feedback, better understand group and team dynamics, and practice the emotional and interpersonal aspects of leadership. Over the years, this tool has been expanded to serve participants at every level of the organization, and some variation has migrated to virtually every American institution.

The T-group and its updated variation, the face-to-face communications laboratory, are often cited as among the best management and leadership learning tools ever conceived. These group dynamics exercises are powerful leadership tools, and there is no better vehicle for building the personal qualities involved in building or recapturing trust.

As originally conceived, the face-to-face communications laboratory required a minimum of two-and-a-half days. In order to accommodate the needs of a broader spectrum of participants, I have developed an alternative program: *the advanced face-to-face communications laboratory*. This streamlined lab is conducted on weekday evenings or on a weekend, at convenient locations. It involves five to ten "strangers" from different organizations.

In order to have the group members get multiple glances at each other's personal and professional style, the lab begins with several paired and group exercises designed to simulate scenarios from the work world, with a rule not to reveal one's educational and/or professional background. Then, the *feedback and critique* portion begins with a matching test, where participants try to figure out who's who. A discussion about why people may have thought one to be "the stock broker," another, "the college professor," another, "the executive," launches the session. Each person is able to find out as much as possible about the impact and impressions that he or she may have made during the course of these highly motivating encounters.

The combination of experienced facilitators and the gradual and appropriate self-disclosure deepens trust, enabling individuals a rare opportunity to explore their most profound and anxiety-filled questions—a chance to ask the other members of the group: Would you buy my product from me? Would you hire me? How would you feel working for (or with) me? Each participant can get the amount of feedback he or she desires. The depth of the critique can be set by the individual, who expresses those issues, dilemmas, and questions he or she wishes to be addressed.

These groups provide people a rare opportunity to find out how others see them, and to take the risk of revealing that which lies beneath their facades, ultimately knowing how others really feel about them and having that feel good.

While this approach provides a. very safe and supportive group climate, I interview all prospective participants to ensure that this experience will be best suited to their developmental needs at the time. I would be pleased to discuss face-to-face communications laboratories with you and answer any questions you may have concerning your particular interests and requirements.

0-595-28765-4

Printed in the United States
35754LVS00004B/307-324